Fingerpower®
Level Four

Effective Technic for All Piano Methods

By John W. Schaum
Edited by Wesley Schaum

T0087293

FOREWORD

Strong fingers are an important requirement for all pianists, amateur and professional. Schaum Fingerpower® exercises are designed to strengthen all five fingers of both hands.

Equal hand development is assured by the performance of the same patterns in each hand, either in parallel motion or with alternating hands. The exercises are purposely short and easily memorized. This enables the student to focus his/her efforts on the technical benefits, listening attentively, and playing with a steady beat.

The exercises become progressively more difficult as the student moves through the book. This makes them an ideal companion to a method book at the same level. The exercises are brief and condensed, so they will easily fit in with a student's other musical assignments. There are opportunities for phrase development, rhythmic variety, and different types of touch.

The series consists of seven books, Primer Level through Level 6.

To access audio, visit:
www.halleonard.com/mylibrary

8661-0358-8643-2838

ISBN 978-1-4950-8200-9

EXCLUSIVELY DISTRIBUTED BY

HAL•LEONARD®

Visit Hal Leonard Online at
www.halleonard.com

Contact Us:
Hal Leonard
7777 West Bluemound Road
Milwaukee, WI 53213
Email: info@halleonard.com

In Europe contact:
Hal Leonard Europe Limited
Distribution Centre, Newmarket Road
Bury St Edmunds, Suffolk, IP33 3YB
Email: info@halleonardeurope.com

In Australia contact:
Hal Leonard Australia Pty. Ltd.
4 Lentara Court
Cheltenham, Victoria, 3192 Australia
Email: info@halleonard.com.au

CONTENTS

PRACTICE SUGGESTIONS

To derive the full benefit from these exercises, they should be played with a firm, solid finger action. **Listen carefully while practicing**. Try to play **each finger equally loud**. Each hand should also play equally loud. It is also important to be aware of the feeling in your fingers and hands during practice.

Each exercise should be practiced four or five times daily, starting at a slow tempo and gradually increasing the tempo as proficiency improves. Several previously learned exercises should be reviewed each week as part of regular practice.

ABOUT THE AUDIO

To access the accompanying audio, go to **www.halleonard.com/mylibrary** and enter the code found on the first page of this book. This will grant you instant access to every example.

There are two tracks for each exercise:
1. Slow practice tempo
2. Performance tempo

The solo part is emphasized on the practice track. The accompaniment is emphasized on the performance track. There are two extra count-in measures before each track.

Follow these three steps for practice variety. At first, the steps should be done with the slow practice tempo. The same steps may be used again at the performance tempo.
1. Student plays right hand only
2. Student plays left hand only
3. Student plays both hands together

1. Legato Interval Etude

2. Tremolo (Wrist Rotation)

3. Rhythmic Wrist Staccato

5

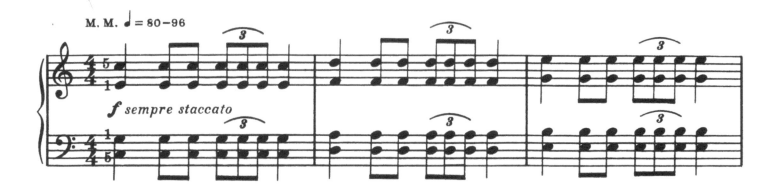

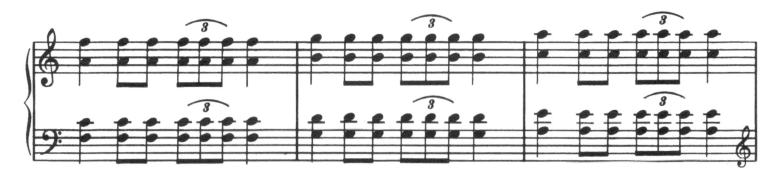

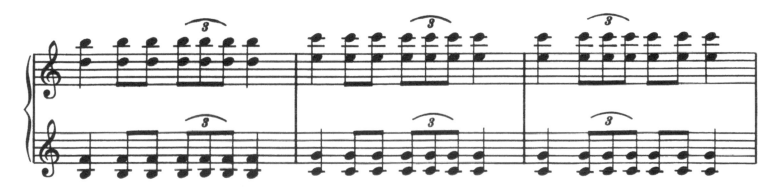

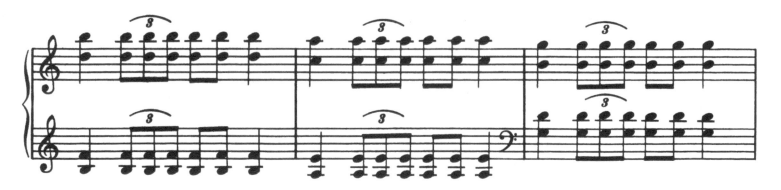

4. Arpeggios in Contrary Motion

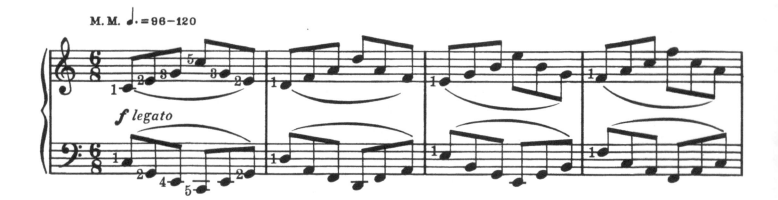

5. Scales in Contrary Motion

M.M. ♩ = 96–112

f legato

6. Thumb Passages

DIRECTIONS: Also play this study in the following patterns:

{ R.H. 1 – 3 – 1 – 3 – 1 – 3   { R.H. 1 – 4 – 1 – 4 – 1 – 4
{ L.H. 1 – 3 – 1 – 3 – 1 – 3   { L.H. 1 – 4 – 1 – 4 – 1 – 4

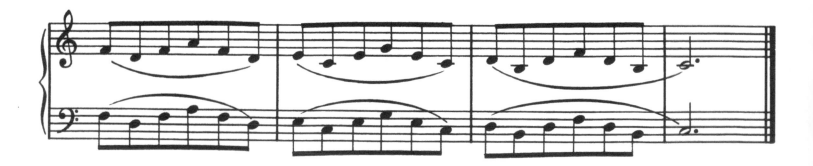

7. Wide Range Finger Etude

8. Two-Octave Arpeggios (Right Hand)

PREPARATORY DRILL

Play strictly legato

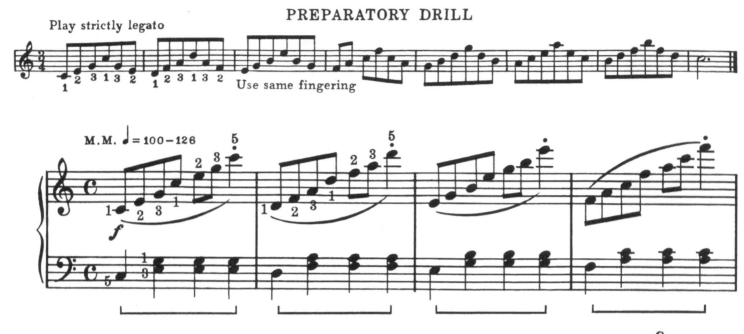

Use same fingering

9. Two-Octave Arpeggios (Left Hand)

PREPARATORY DRILL

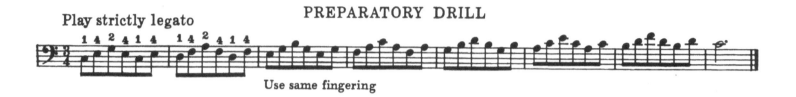

Play strictly legato

Use same fingering

M.M. ♩ = 100–126

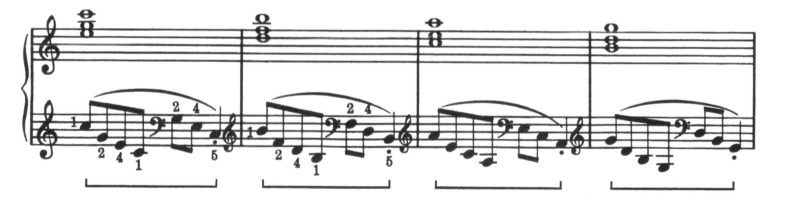

10. Arpeggios in Triplets

11. Sustained Thirds

13

Note: Play slowly, and strike each finger firmly, the whole note must be strictly held.

M. M. ♩ = 66 – 88

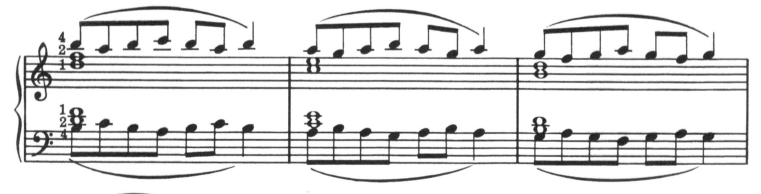

12. Major Triad Inversions

M. M. ♩ = 88–112

13. Arpeggio Inversions

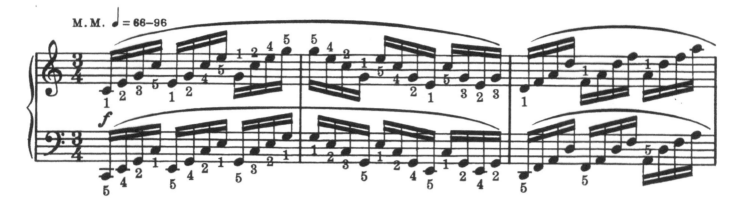

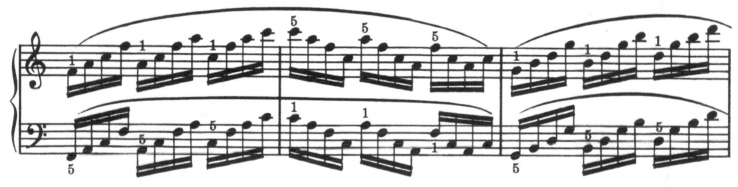

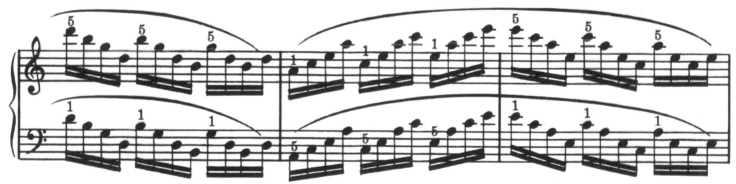

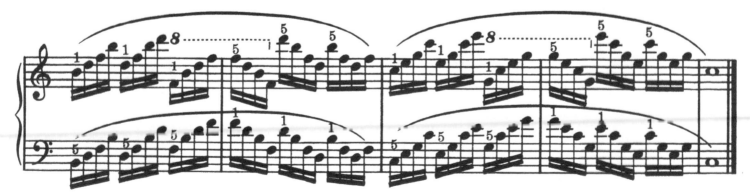

14. Trills in Thirds

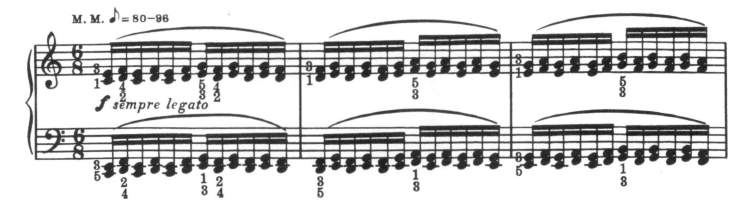

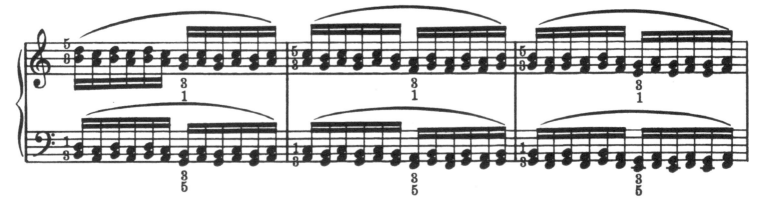

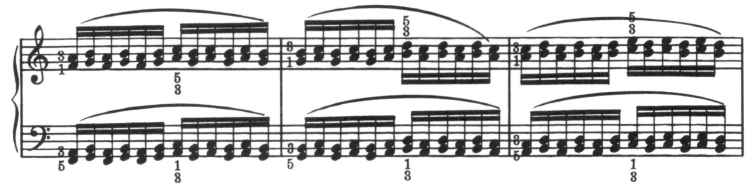

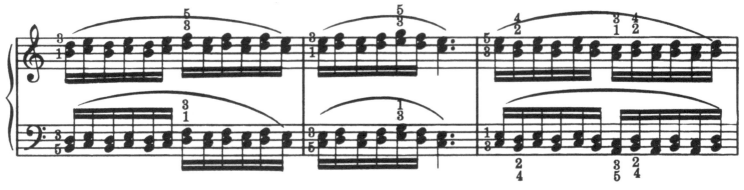

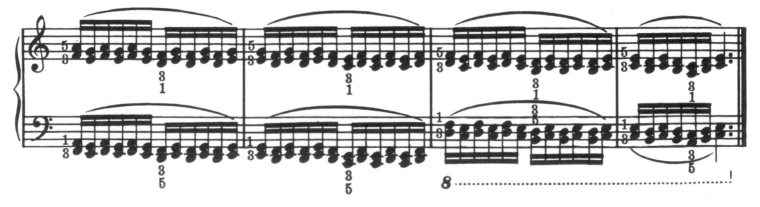

15. Triplet Trills

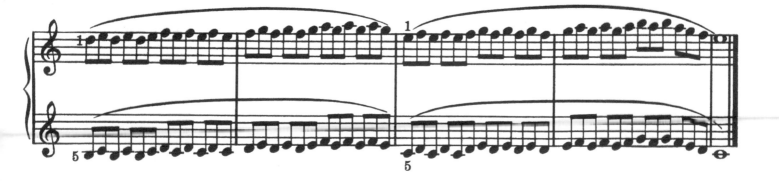

18

16. Double Grace Notes

The quarter notes should be strongly accented.

M.M. ♩=66-76

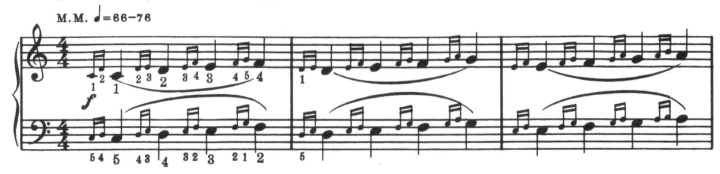

17. Chromatic Hand Contractions

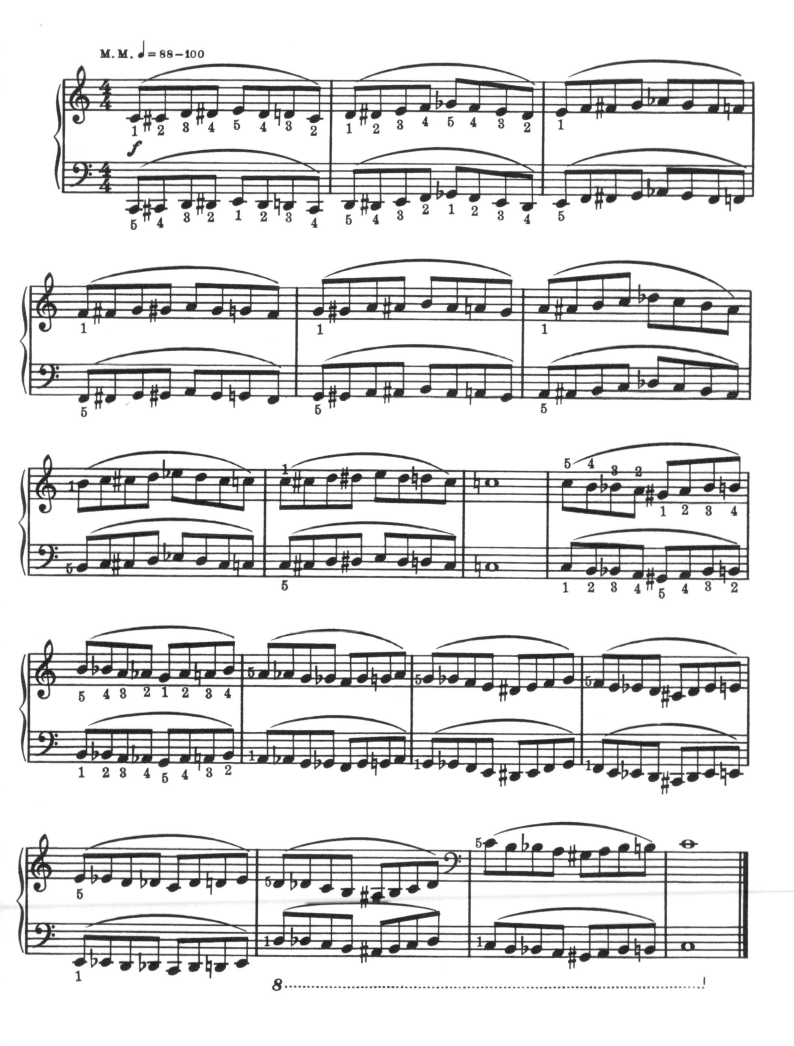

18. Finger Expansion

The patterns for Etude numbers 18 and 19 are derived from the diminished seventh chord. Study the following examples.

Dim. 7 — Pattern for Etude No. 18 — Pattern for Etude No. 19

M.M. ♩ = 104–126

19. Equalization of the Fingers

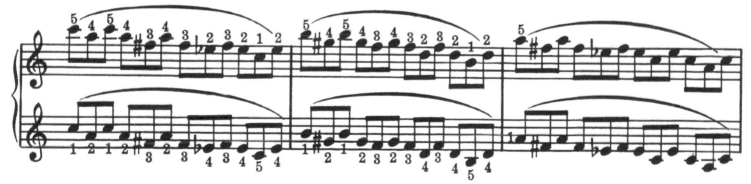

20. Four-Finger Dexterity

The thumbs are to be omitted throughout this Etude.

M.M. ♩ = 50–80

21. Legato Triads and Thirds

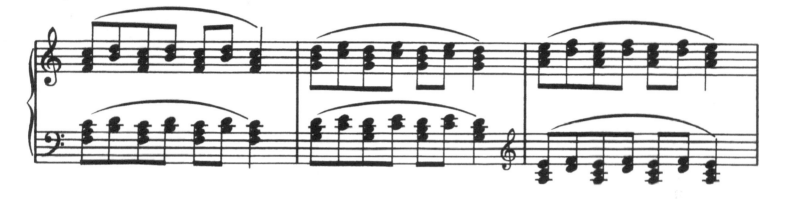

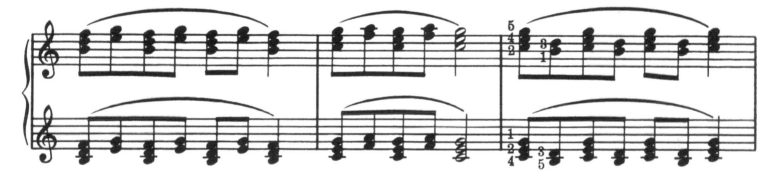

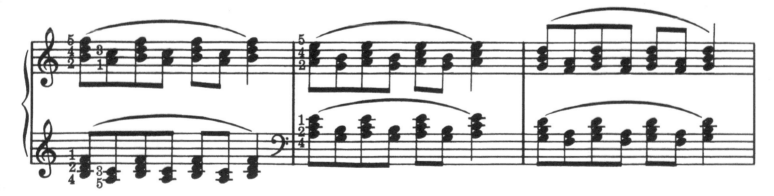

You are now ready to progress to Schaum **FINGERPOWER**, Level Five.

MORE GREAT SCHAUM PUBLICATIONS

FINGERPOWER®

by John W. Schaum
Physical training and discipline
are needed for both athletics and
keyboard playing. Keyboard muscle
conditioning is called technic.
Technic exercises are as important
to the keyboard player as workouts
and calisthenics are to the athlete.
Schaum's *Fingerpower®* books
are dedicated to development
of individual finger strength and
dexterity in both hands.

00645334	Primer Level – Book Only	$6.99
00645016	Primer Level – Book/Audio	$8.99
00645335	Level 1 – Book Only	$6.99
00645019	Level 1 – Book/Audio	$7.99
00645336	Level 2 – Book Only	$6.99
00645022	Level 2 – Book/Audio	$7.99
00645337	Level 3 – Book Only	$6.95
00645025	Level 3 – Book/Audio	$7.99
00645338	Level 4 – Book Only	$6.99
00645028	Level 4 – Book/Audio	$8.99
00645339	Level 5 Book Only	$6.99
00645340	Level 6 Book Only	$6.99

FINGERPOWER® ETUDES

Melodic exercises crafted by master
technic composers. Modified or
transposed etudes provide equal
hand development with a planned
variety of technical styles, key, and
time signatures.

00645392	Primer Level	$6.95
00645393	Level 1	$6.99
00645394	Level 2	$6.99
00645395	Level 3	$6.95
00645396	Level 4	$6.99

FINGERPOWER® FUN

arr. Wesley Schaum
Early Elementary Level
Musical experiences beyond the
traditional *Fingerpower®* books that
include fun to play pieces with finger
exercises and duet accompaniments.
Short technic prepartory drills (finger
workouts) focus on melodic patterns
found in each piece.

00645126	Primer Level	$6.95
00645127	Level 1	$6.95
00645128	Level 2	$6.95
00645129	Level 3	$6.95
00645144	Level 4	$6.95

FINGERPOWER POP

Arranged by James Poteat
10 great pop piano solo
arrangements with fun technical
warm-ups that complement the
Fingerpower series! Can also be used
as motivating supplements to any
method and in any learning situation.

00237508	Primer Level	$9.99
00237510	Level 1	$9.99
00282865	Level 2	$9.99

FINGERPOWER® TRANSPOSER

by Wesley Schaum
Early Elementary Level
This book includes 21 short,
8-measure exercises using 5-finger
patterns. Positions are based on C,F,
and G major and no key signatures
are used. Patterns involve intervals
of 3rds, 4ths, and 5ths up and down
and are transposed from C to F and
F to C, C to G and G to C, G to F and
F to G.

00645150	Primer Level	$6.95
00645151	Level 1	$6.95
00645152	Level 2	$6.95
00645154	Level 3	$6.95
00645156	Level 4	$6.95

JUMBO STAFF MANUSCRIPT BOOK

This pad features 24 pages with 4
staves per page.
00645936 .... $4.25

CERTIFICATE OF MUSICAL ACHIEVEMENT

Reward your students for their hard
work with these official 8x10 inch
certificates that you can customize.
12 per package.
00645938 .... $6.99

SCHAUM LESSON ASSIGNMENT BOOK

by John Schaum
With space for 32 weeks, this book
will help keep students on the right
track for their practice time.
00645935 .... $3.95

www.halleonard.com

Prices, contents, and availability subject to change without notice.